SNOOPY'S VERY FIRST CHRISTMAS SONGS

CONTENTS

Copyright © 1989 by HOUSTON PUBLISHING, INC., 224 S. Lebanon St., Lebanon, IN 46052
All rights reserved. International Copyright Secured. Printed in the USA

JOLLY OLD ST. NICHOLAS

Jol - ly old St. Ni - cho - las lean your ear this way ; don't you tell a sin - gle soul

2.

what I'm going to say ; Christ - mas Eve is

com - ing soon, now you dear old man

whis - per what you'll bring to me, tell me if you can.

3.

GOOD KING WENCESLAS

4.

deep and crisp and ev - en. Bright - ly shone the

moon that night, though the frost was cru - el, When a poor man

came in sight, gath - 'ring win - ter fu - el.

5.

WE THREE KINGS

We three Kings of O - ri - ent are,

Bear - ing gifts we tra - verse a - far,

Field and foun - tain, moor and moun - tain, fol - low - ing

6.

yon - der star. Oh, _____ Star of

won - der, star of might; Star with ra - dient

beau - ty bright; West - ward lead - ing still pro -

ceed - ing, guide us to the per - fect light.

7.

JINGLE BELLS

Jin - gle bells, jin - gle bells, jin - gle all the

way; Oh what fun it is to ride in a

8.

one — horse op - en sleigh! _____ Jin - gle bells,

jin - gle bells, jin - gle all the way;

Oh what fun it is to ride in a one—horse op - en sleigh!

9.

UP ON THE HOUSETOP

Up on the house-top rein-deer pause, out jumps good old

San-ta Claus, load-ed all down with lots of toys, all for the lit-tle ones

10.

11.

GOD REST YE MERRY GENTLEMEN

God rest ye mer-ry gen-tle-men let noth-ing you dis-

may, Re - mem-ber Christ our Sa - vior was born on Christ-mas

Day, To save us all from Sa - tan's pow'r when we have gone a -

stray. Oh, ___ tid - ings of com - fort and joy, com-fort and

joy, Oh, ___ tid - ings of com - fort and joy.

13.

Dear Mary Christmas,
Congratulations on deciding
to keep your own name.

AWAY IN A MANGER

R.H. 1 2 3 4

G A B C D E F G

L.H. 4 3 2 1

A - way ____ in a man - ger no crib for a

bed ; The lit - tle Lord Je - sus lay

14.

down His sweet head . The stars ——— in the

Hea - ven look down where He lay ; The

lit - tle Lord Je - sus a - sleep in the hay .

O LITTLE TOWN OF BETHLEHEM

O lit - tle town of Beth - le - hem , how still we __ see thee

lie , A - bove thy deep and dream - less sleep the

si - lent stars go by ; Yet in thy dark streets shin - eth the ev - er - last - ing light , The hopes and fears of all the years are met in thee to - night .

JOY TO THE WORLD

Joy to the world! The Lord has come. Let earth re-ceive her King. Let ev-ry heart _____ pre - pare __ Him __ room , _____ And

Heav'n and na - ture __ sing , and __ Heav'n and na - ture __ sing , and __

Heav'n __ and Heav'n _____ and na - ture sing .

19.

ROCKING CAROL

Ma - ry's lit - tle new born Son, safe from harm,

slum - ber now with - out a - larm. Lit - tle lamb of God come down, from a - bove, to all_Earth His_ gift of_love. While we rock you, rock you, rock you,

while we rock you, rock you, rock you, Grant that we our whole lives_through, find our_joy in_

serv - ing_you.

O COME, ALL YE FAITHFUL

Come and be - hold Him, Born the King of an - gels; O

come let us a - dore Him, O come let us a - dore Him, O

come let us a - dore Him ___ Christ, ___ the Lord.

23.

THE FIRST NOEL

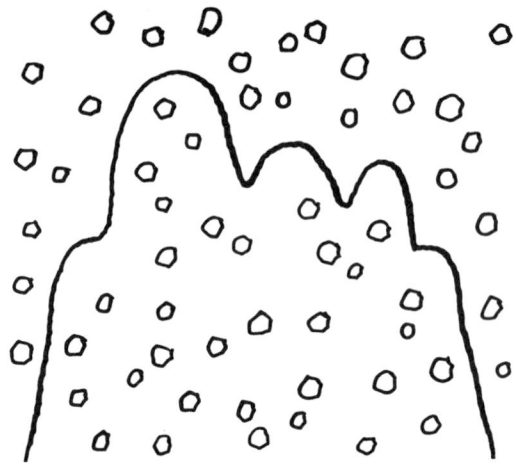

The— first____ no - el , the— an - gels did say , was to cer - tain poor shep - herds in fields where they lay ; In__ fields____ where__

24.

they lay___ keep - ing their sheep, on a cold win - ter's night___ that

was___ so deep. No - el, _____ no - el, no - el, no -

el. Born is the King___ of Is - ra - el.

25.

WE WISH YOU A MERRY CHRISTMAS

We wish you a mer-ry Christ-mas. We wish you a mer-ry Christ-mas. We wish you a mer-ry Christ-mas, and a

26.

ha - py New Year. Good ti - dings we bring to you and your friends. We wish you a mer - ry Christ - mas and a hap - py New Year.

SILENT NIGHT

Si - lent night, ho - ly night.

All is calm, all is bright. 'Round yon

Vir - gin, Moth - er and Child, Ho - ly
In - fant so ten - der and mild, Sleep in heav - en - ly
peace, _____ sleep _____ in heav - en - ly peace. _____

29.

DECK THE HALLS

Deck___ the halls with | boughs of hol - ly, | Fa la la la la___ la

la la la ; | 'Tis___ the sea - son | to be jol - ly,

30.

Fa la la la la_____ la la la la; Don____ we now our

gay___ ap - par - el, Fa la la, fa la la, la la la;

Troll___ the an - cient yule - tide ca - rol, Fa la la la la_____ la la la la.

PEANUTS PIANO COURSE

A new series of 14 course and supplementary books featuring the world acclaimed PEANUTS characters of Charles M. Schulz. An obvious delight for students of all ages.

THE PEANUTS PIANO COURSE
by June Edison

High level pedagogy presented in straight-forward simplicity. Author June Edison has created a course that is *right* for teachers of all backgrounds. The **PEANUTS** characters participate in the teaching process in a way that provides the epitome of motivation for effective instruction.

Houston PUBLISHING INC.

224 South Lebanon Street
Lebanon, IN 46052
317/ 482-4440
800/ 992-6676

PEANUTS Piano Course

___	P01	PEANUTS Piano Course - Book 1	$5.50
___	P02	PEANUTS Piano Course - Book 2	$5.50
___	P03	PEANUTS Piano Course - Book 3	$5.50
___	P04	PEANUTS Piano Course - Book 4	$5.50
___	P05	PEANUTS Piano Course - Book 5	$5.50
___	P06	PEANUTS Piano Course - Book 6	$5.50
___	P11	PEANUTS First Program Book	$5.50
___	P12	PEANUTS Second Program Book	$5.50
___	P13	PEANUTS Snoopy's Very First Christmas Songs	$5.50